The BLANK JOURNAL

Biking in all 50 States and So Much More

BOB AND TAMMY CRANSTON

WestBow Press books may be ordered through booksellers or by contacting:

WestBow Press
A Division of Thomas Nelson & Zondervan
1663 Liberty Drive
Bloomington, IN 47403
www.westbowpress.com
844-714-3454

ISBN: 978-1-6642-9429-5 (sc)
ISBN: 978-1-6642-9430-1 (hc)
ISBN: 978-1-6642-9428-8 (e)

Library of Congress Control Number: 2023905186

Print information available on the last page.

WestBow Press rev. date: 03/27/2023

WESTBOW
PRESS®
A DIVISION OF THOMAS NELSON
& ZONDERVAN

Contents

Chapter One
CHANGE

━━━◦✦◦━━━

The black leather journal sat open-faced on the table showcasing its blank sheets of paper. The clean slate reminded us of the inevitable constant in life–change. A new journey had begun for us. At 57 (Bob) and 51 (Tammy) years of age, we started anew. Our lives as we once knew them took an "about face," forcing us to march in a different direction. The blank journal represented the unknown–our unwritten story. With God's blessings, we pressed onward, emotional wounds and all, as we embraced our future.

Feeling like battle-scarred warriors, with aging bodies, we agreed to set goals and to pursue lifelong dreams. We determined to fill the currently empty journal with a record of our future travels and accomplishments. Ink would record details that might otherwise be forgotten. Through journals, pictures, and videos, the memories would forever be etched in our minds. We welcomed our partnership and future with vigor. We had lofty intentions to "go, see, and do."

A blank paper has a significant, personal meaning. After we repeated the traditional "Do you promise…? Do you take…? I Do's…" on April 7, 2012, in Champaign, Illinois, the pastor presented us with a blank sheet of paper. During the ceremony, he stated, "Bob and Tammy know what it is like to live out the vows to be faithful through sickness and health." Each of us had lost our previous spouse to cancer–unfortunate loss changed us. Time, relationships, and memories now had heightened value. When we signed the blank sheet of paper, it testified of God's goodness. We trusted Him, the author of new beginnings, to write our story.

We met at a hospice-sponsored grief support group. Through shared tears, we acknowledged our loss. We worked through our grief, setting an intention to heal, which really meant learning to live with our grief, and we sought to find a "new normal" during the difficult transition. We were not in denial, and we were not angry. We knew our lives would never be the same. We were in the acceptance stage of grief. We could never go back to the lives we once knew, nor could we stay where we were, so we pushed forward through the eight-step process.

Near the end of the two-month long program, our leader instructed us to make a list. She wanted us to put serious thought into our lists of activities we had always wanted to do but had never pursued. We cannot recall everything we wrote on our individual lists, but two things on Tammy's list come to mind because they came to fruition–to obtain a college degree and to take ballroom dance lessons. Surprisingly, Bob showed interest in dance lessons as well. Individually, we registered online for the beginner class, Ballroom 101.

Ballroom dance lessons at Regent Ballroom in Champaign, Illinois

In a very different setting, we began to meet on Tuesday evenings at the Regent Ballroom and Dance Center in Savoy, Illinois. We stepped out of our comfort zones and challenged ourselves. Burdened bodies lightened when brand-new, leather-soled shoes made contact on a smooth dance floor. The change in tempo refreshed us. Sorrow turned to joy.

Experiencing all the "firsts" after the deaths of our spouses was extremely difficult. Everything was a first–staring at the empty chair across the table, going to church alone, missing them during holidays, and even mundane things like receiving mail with their name on it. Taking dance lessons was a big first step in a positive direction for both of us, no pun intended. Understandably, emotions were all over the place. We felt skepticism and excitement, hope and despair. Our feelings were on opposite ends of the spectrum from one minute to the next. But through it all, we encouraged each other to talk, and we felt validated when we did. Who else could understand?

We would not allow grief to consume us to the point that it would rob us of future joy. We stood firmly on the dance floor with heads up, shoulders back, and arms locked. The elegant posture concealed our broken spirits. To the count of 1-2-3, 1-2-3, back-side-together, front-side-together, our feet merged into a box step. Eventually smiles appeared, followed by laughter. We laughed at ourselves, and we laughed at each other as we struggled to put into practice the instructors' guidance. They made every movement flow gracefully, but simple it was not! For a moment we were overcome with a dash of guilt. "Is it too soon to smile?" we wondered. Of course not! This was what Larry and Barb would have wanted. A flicker of joy resurfaced. Through ballroom dancing, dinner dates, weekend hikes, prayers, counseling, and deep conversations, a love story evolved.

When we began developing wedding plans, it didn't take long to choose the venue for our wedding reception. It had to be the dance hall. We settled on a wedding date according to availability. The wedding celebration combined families, friends, and close relatives of our deceased spouses. We requested no gifts. We already had two households full of belongings that we would need to merge into one space. In lieu of gifts, we purchased small clipboards which we placed on each table with a cream-colored card stock titled, "Notes to Bob & Tammy." We asked our guests to write advice or to share whatever was on their hearts. Many of these messages are priceless to us:

Aunt Mary said, "Be sure to have your camera handy and use it often. I always cherish your pictures."

Sheryl said, "As you know full well, marriage is a lifelong endeavor, and who would be more 'in tune' to sharing that than two people who have already shown that kind of faithfulness…till death do us part?"

Donna said, "As a couple and as individuals, your candor and transparency is so refreshing. But what stands out the most is your true character and how God was faithful in your time of need as you were faithful to Him."

Lisa said, "Tonight our prayers have been answered. We want to be a part of this new journey. You and Bob are now Aunt Tammy and Uncle Bob."

These snippets captured what was important to us–our faith, our friends, and our family. We aim to be transparent. It remains our hope and purpose to encourage, uplift, and inspire.

On a deep level, we understand the fragility of life. We have succumbed to the reality that things could turn on a dime at any moment. Though newlyweds, we were fully aware that, in all probability, one of us would go through the difficult task of burying a loved one, once again. In contrast to that thought, we also felt empowered. God carried us through difficult times in the past, and we were certain that he would faithfully do it again. God's provision in the past provided hope for our future!

Chapter Two

IN PURSUIT

Creating a bucket list was one of our first goal-oriented activities together, and we discussed it at length. What were new things we could do together? Where, in our wildest dreams, would we like to go? Where would we retire? Like us, the list is a continual work in progress. In our new black travel journal, Bob finally penned a short list, "Run a 5K together, publish Tammy's book, complete at least 25 years at Carle Foundation Hospital, vacation in Canada, Africa, Australia, New Zealand, and Asia, and lastly, bike together." We later defined the biking goal as riding our tandem together in all fifty states. As late-in-life newlyweds, we excitedly set out to pursue our life-long dreams.

Both of us have always been goal setters, and together we focused on setting common goals as the first step towards our desired future. We did not want to live adrift. A life without vision or purpose seemed meaningless to us. God placed us on this earth at a specific time, for specific tasks. Our job is to use the gifts and talents he has given us to do the work he will bless. In the grand scheme of things, we hope that people within our circle of influence are positively touched. We enjoy learning new things, spending time with family, and seeking new experiences, and goals help us do these things with intentionality.

Tammy promoting hospice volunteering

Due to Tammy's personal experience with hospice, she set a goal to become a hospice volunteer. The compassion, care, and support she experienced with the hospice team inspired her to pay it forward. After specialized training, she was able to personally assist many families in their grieving process. She co-led grief support groups and worked one-on-one with patients, getting them involved in creating their own, personal memorial DVDs. It was especially rewarding when she could encourage patients to record video messages or write letters as a last gift to their families.

Another major undertaking Tammy planned was writing a book about God's support and faithfulness through the journey of Larry's illness and death. After lots of work, many revisions, and reaching out to multiple publishers, *Why Not Me?* was published by Teach Services, Inc. God used her experiences, abilities, and voice to encourage others and glorify Him.

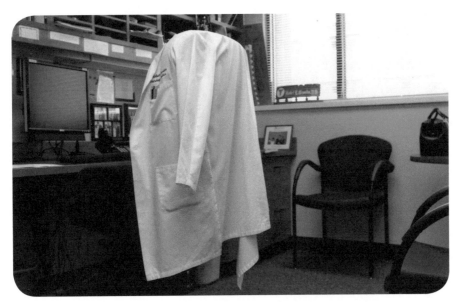

Bob's medical office in the Neurology Department

Earlier in life, God had led Bob into and through medical school and advanced training. He had felt called to this vocation based on his desire to help other people and his joy in learning about the human body. God also helped Bob establish a palliative medicine program and an internal professional coaching department at Carle Foundation Hospital. Both undertakings were long processes, but God guided and supported him through the endeavors.

Our major goals these days are to assist and encourage our combined family and grandchildren. We spend as much time with them as we can, hoping to be good examples, a constant support, and a godly influence.

It is our hope that those who come behind us find us faithful. What could be a greater legacy? At this stage in our lives, our mission is to finish well and have some fun along the way.

The skills Tammy acquired while pursuing a degree in communication, with a focus on photography, videography, and writing, proved highly useful in documenting our journey together. Bob recorded the who, what, where, when, and why on previously blank pages in the black journal, and then after each trip, we worked together on a Shutterfly book combining words with pictures to capture the details of the journey. We often joke about admiring our collection of books when we are older, sitting in rocking chairs, saying, "We did this! We went there!" Our collection includes vacations with family, bike trips, mission trips, and international travels. While the Shutterfly books are detailed historical records, this book will focus on our experiences, thoughts, and feelings while pursuing the goal to ride our tandem bicycle in all fifty states. A chronology of the actual bike trips can be found at the end of the book.

A great advantage of riding the tandem together is that we can easily talk. We share observations about the ride–unusual things we see, picturesque vistas, and the quality of the trail. Additionally, we talk about other issues on our hearts and minds.

The Blank Journal is about our cherished time together through shared adventures, discoveries, obstacles, accomplishments, and conversations while achieving our goal. We also share some of the unexpected surprises along the way. We aimed to ride at least twenty miles in each of the fifty states, but under extreme conditions, our minimum was ten miles per state. As a secondary goal, we planned to visit as many county, state, and national parks as possible.

Chapter Three
BREAKTHROUGHS AND DISCOVERIES

Our beautiful tandem recumbent bicycle

Our ten-foot-long, navy-blue Sun tandem has recumbent seats with independent pedaling. Though it is a "semi" of a bike, it is very comfortable. Frequently, we bike, load up, spend the night, and move on. Most planned bike trips include at least three locations, but the longer trips included up to seven states.

In August of 2013, we planned a week-long Cape Cod biking and touring trip. As usual, the trip was planned far in advance. Close to our departure date, we received an unexpected phone call which would alter our plans. Bob's deceased wife's father had passed away. We both wanted to be in Phoenix for the memorial service but after serious consideration, we decided to divide and conquer. With the plan to reunite in Massachusetts, Bob flew to Arizona while Tammy embarked on the longest road trip she had ever undertaken by herself. Though she began the trip with some trepidation, she accomplished it without any difficulties.

As she passed through Buffalo, New York, she realized how close she was to Niagara Falls. She decided on the spur of the moment to detour and visit this international park.

Entering Cape Cod in 2013, one of our early extended bike trips

When Tammy approached Cape Cod, a billboard caught her attention. She made another spontaneous decision to visit the Cape Cod Butterfly House. She could photograph butterflies without feeling rushed. Later that evening, Tammy picked up Bob from the Cape Cod Airfield in Marston Mills, Massachusetts. Bob was glad to see her and proud that she made the 1,129-mile, 18-hour trip on her own without a hitch. Tammy's planning for this vacation was salvaged.

The marsh field we waded through

Tammy loves photographing lighthouses. On this trip, we biked the peninsula and photographed eight lighthouses all together. Some were easier to find than others. At Herring Cove, a ranger gave us directions to walk approximately one mile to reach the Race Point Lighthouse. We estimated the walk was closer to three miles, and we were not informed we would need to wade through a marsh field to get close enough to photograph the lighthouse. Tammy's shorts were soaked, but Bob, being taller, was knee deep. After our trek, wet and hungry, Tammy held her shorts out the window to dry so we could get a bite to eat.

The West Chop Lighthouse on Martha's Vineyard

We also rode the ferry to Martha's Vineyard and completed a twenty-mile ride on the enchanting island. We were impressed with the smooth bike trail, often along the seashore, with well-marked signage. Tammy photographed the West Chop Lighthouse and East Chop Lighthouse while Bob kept track of the time, making sure we had time to eat dinner before catching the return ferry.

Standing by Mayflower II, full-size replica of the Mayflower

During our stay in Cape Cod, we toured national landmarks. The historical Plymouth Rock, the replica of the Mayflower, and the National Monument to the Forefathers gave us a deep appreciation for the hardships the pilgrims endured. Forty-five of the 102 Mayflower passengers died in the winter of 1620-1621. Standing reverently at this monument, we were in awe of the challenges they faced, and we left thankful for the estimated 35 million people worldwide who have descended from the Pilgrims. An interesting historical point we learned was that they originally landed across the bay at Provincetown. The ground was not good for crops, and there wasn't enough water to sustain them, so the next season they fled to Plymouth for more arable land and plenteous water. After an interesting week of day trips in the area, including an outstanding three-hour whale watching excursion, our trip home was uneventful.

While researching trails, we discovered that occasionally we were able to bike two states in one day as we did on the Chief Ladiga Trail in Alabama, followed by the Silver Comet Trail in Georgia. Together, the combined trails cover nearly 100 miles, but after we biked forty miles, we rewarded ourselves with soft serve ice cream at the end of the day.

On the Hiawatha Trail

Another example of a trail that connects two states is the scenic Hiawatha Trail, which starts at the Montana state line but crosses into Idaho. The Hiawatha Trail, a rail to trail bike path, originally had been designated as one of the most scenic rail trips in America. Due to the long train tunnels, which required a bicycle light, and the roughness of some of the gravel path, we rented a tandem for this ride. The views were spectacular as we crossed seven sky-high trestles which showcased picturesque ravines. It was a relatively easy ride, coasting down a slow fifteen-mile descent. Later that day we rode the Coeur d'Alene Trail for an additional flat, fifteen miles along the marsh field.

Franconia Notch State Park, New Hampshire

In contrast, the trail in Franconia Notch State Park in New Hampshire was anything but flat. The trail was so hilly, following the lay of the land, that we were forced to dismount several times to push the bike. Our total distance that day was less than fifteen miles.

Some trails, like the Eastern Promenade Trail in Portland, Maine, had unexpected surprises. We enjoyed the waterfront scenery for miles, until we rode past a stinky waste processing plant. To get in our twenty miles we had to pass the plant twice, plugging our noses the second time.

"Leaf peeping" at Roger Williams Park

In Cranston, Rhode Island, we looked forward to biking the Cranston Bike Path since it bears our name. Disappointingly, we discovered this was possibly the worst trail of our fifty states. Our main challenge was dodging litter on our 20-mile ride. Graffiti and broken fences added to the overall rundown condition. Even the trail sign itself needed repair. We planned the trip around the fall foliage season, and even though we were about a week early, the leaves at Roger Williams Park were stunning. The park came highly recommended for "leaf peeping," as referred to by the locals. We were not aware that such a term even existed. River Birch, Ginkgo, Japanese Maple, Sweet Gum, and Sugar Maple (at the Iron Bridge) were some of the trees we peeped and photographed.

Chapter Four

ADVENTURERS

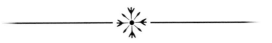

During the northeast bike trip, we spent a day at Acadia National Park. This is a place we plan to return to. In an Internet search, Tammy admired pictures of Cobblestone Beach. She printed directions from a blog post about how to best access the beach. We found out for ourselves it wasn't a marked path, and it didn't take long to realize we needed to crawl on the wet, rounded, cobblestone rocks rather than walk upright.

Jordan's Pond, Acadia National Park, a peaceful retreat

One of the most picturesque locations at Acadia was Jordan's Pond, where the water was clear and as smooth as glass. Sitting beside the still water was calming and refreshing. Someday when we return, we hope to hike the 3.3-mile Jordan Pond Shore Trail.

An adventurous bike ride occurred at Hilton Head, South Carolina. It was a beautiful ride around an alligator infested pond which included three different beach sites. On this ride, though, we unwittingly broke a series of rules. We biked through a residential neighborhood to one of the beach sites, where a sign informed us we were trespassing. We accidentally biked the wrong direction down several one-way streets, and we inadvertently parked our van in an illegal location. Bob suggested, "We are breaking so many rules, we might as well go skinny dipping." Tammy laughed but vetoed that idea.

High Bridge Trail in Farmville, Virginia, a historic Civil War site

On another ride in Virginia, we were short on time as we had arranged to meet Bob's younger brother, John, for dinner. We changed our clothes in the van, in a downtown parking lot before accessing the High Bridge Trail in Farmville. We biked faster than usual on the hard-packed gravel with the goal to reach the historic, majestic High Bridge. It is more than 2,400 feet long and 125 feet above the Appomattox River. Despite our rush, Tammy scaled the safety fence to seize the opportunity to get the best possible photograph of the bridge. Returning to the car, we quickly disassembled the bike, wiped sweat off our brows, and changed our clothes once again before speeding off to catch up with John. We ate dinner at Junction, a rustic farm-to-table, southwestern restaurant in Charlottesville. Tammy swore that the vegetable quesadillas were the best she had ever eaten. After a great two-hour visit with John, we drove through the dark countryside, carefully avoiding twelve deer on our way back to camp.

Glamping at Sandy River Outdoor Adventure, in Rice, Virginia

Of all the places we have stayed while biking, Sandy River Outdoor Adventure in Rice, Virginia, deserves special recognition. What was so noteworthy about it? Not only did they have well-equipped cabins for rent, but they also had "glamour" teepees with all the bells and whistles: queen size bed, heat and air, kitchenette, tiled walk-in shower, rustic wooden table, and a large, flat screened TV. Not your typical teepee! The campground also featured an outdoor tree obstacle course with high ropes and bridges. Tammy immediately decided this would be a great place to bring the entire family in a few years to celebrate her sixtieth birthday.

Wanting to capture memories, Tammy talked Bob into sitting on the hammock together near the outdoor fire pit, complete with a massive kettle to cook meals in. Tammy often sets up her tripod and uses the timer feature on her camera. In this instance, however, a ten-second delay did not give her enough time to successfully join Bob in the hammock. She pushed the button, ran, slid into the hammock, and as the shutter clicked, the photo showed Bob and Tammy falling out of the hammock unto the ground, laughing. After three attempts and several bruises, we got our keepsake snapshot.

Our first encounter with a large, wild animal on Tony Knowles Coastal Trail

Biking in Anchorage, Alaska, on the Tony Knowles Coastal Trail, brought a unique twist on trail riding. We enjoyed the flat, paved trail with beautiful trees and shrubbery with occasional glimpses of the Cook Inlet. While pedaling along on a rented tandem, we noticed several bikers stopped ahead of us on the trail. A biker that crossed us said, "There's a moose up ahead." We pedaled with eyes wide open. Tammy longed for a picture of a moose! Bob was the first to notice a large brown head peeking over the tall brush to the left of the trail. We dismounted, tried to keep our distance, shooting video and taking pictures with the brush obscuring our view. Suddenly, the moose stepped out of the brush and onto the trail less than twenty feet from Tammy. In the meantime, two police officers had arrived on bike, and Tammy felt comfortable continuing to shoot. This was the first big wild animal we had encountered on a bike trail. One of the officers estimated that he weighed 700 to 800 pounds. The officer said that the moose would likely gain another 100 pounds before the cold weather set in.

Likewise, in Hawaii, we rented a tandem. Because of the many hills in what is deemed the most unfriendly bicycle state, the bike shop clerk advised us to rent an electric bike. The electric motor augments the efforts of the riders. We pedaled continuously but opted to use the power assist when scaling hills or needing a quick acceleration to avoid pedestrians.

We biked on a curvy trail and a few streets until we reached the Lahaina Banyan Tree which is one of the country's largest banyan trees. Planted across the street from the city courthouse this sprawling tree is the size of an entire city block and provides much needed shade to the community.

Sporting our new t-shirts under the large banyan tree

Underneath the large branches of the amazing tree, we stopped to rest and take pictures. Suddenly, we heard screaming, "Does anyone have an Epi-pen? We need an Epi-pen!" A young woman was having a food-related anaphylactic reaction in the restaurant across the street. Bob always carries an Epi-pen on the bike, and he immediately offered it in this life-threatening emergency. Bob waved and passed his Epi-pen to the screaming man who took off running like he had been handed a baton in a relay race. Bob followed him into the restaurant, but by the time he got there, emergency medical assistance had arrived. Fortunately, the woman survived the reaction, and Bob was able to recover his unused Epi-pen.

Tammy, relieved, had been concerned about Bob not having it available for use should he need it. Bob has a history of rare but serious food-related, exercise-induced anaphylaxis. On one occasion many years ago, he was hospitalized overnight for a bad reaction. Fortunately, on our bike trips so far, we have not had to use the Epi-pen because we make sure he doesn't ride within two hours of eating, a measure that usually prevents the reactions from occurring. However, on a few hikes, the welts appeared, breathing tightened, and his tongue began to swell. The Epi-pen was administered in the anterior thigh to successfully abort the attack.

All dressed up for the Old Lahaina Luau

Our trip to Hawaii also provided some unique adventures outside of our biking experience. In Maui, we attended the Old Lahaina Luau, watched a baby whale breach while on a whale watching tour, walked four miles on the beautiful Kapalua Coastal Trail, and drove our rented jeep on the Road to Hana. At the Wai'anapanapa State Park, we stepped on the beautiful black sand and lava rocks as we walked the Pi'ilani Trail. On our return trip, we took the rugged southern, back-country road. Tammy stood up in her seat to capture video and pictures through the sunroof.

In Oahu, we rented a Camry which was much cheaper than the $50 a day surcharge for the jeep. We stayed at the Hilton Hawaiian Village, which ironically, charged $50 a day for parking. We experienced close-up encounters with green sea turtles on a pre-arranged Turtle Canyon Catamaran Snorkel cruise from Waikiki. Planning for our next three days we decided to pay for an "Ocean One" cage-free shark experience, complete with photo package. Tammy reluctantly agreed to participate in this venture because this was a scientific team who had a 100 percent safety record. We now have treasured pictures from this once in a lifetime, death-defying excursion.

The dangerous and strenuous Koko Crater Trail

Interestingly, the truly most dangerous experience occurred because a relatively safe hike up the Diamond Head Trail was closed due to renovations. Through a search, Bob found Koko Crater Trail which was nearby. Upon our arrival, we were surprised to see several signs that warned of danger, but because we saw many people on the trail, we decided to try it.

It was a difficult uphill hike on an old tram track used during World War II to haul supplies up the steep hill to military pillboxes. It was a strenuous climb, with wide steps and loose dirt. Tammy, who rarely perspires, was a sweaty mess when we reached the top. We took a quick photo to show we conquered the uphill climb and immediately began our descent as dusk approached. The loose dirt caused the footing to be more challenging on the downhill journey, and after Tammy slid, we decided to scoot on our butts from one crosstie to the next until we passed the steepest part of the trail. Tammy was disappointed as she realized she was ruining one of her favorite pair of capris but hoped to get off the trail safely to have the opportunity to shop again!

Providentially, as darkness set in, a fellow walker stayed with us and escorted us down the hill with his bright flashlight. We encouraged him to go around us because we knew this would be a long ordeal. But he said, "I don't have anywhere I need to be." We talked about his divorce, children, and personal adventurers until we safely reached the bottom. We discovered he was a man of faith, and we thanked him profusely, prayed with him about the trials he was going through, and called him "our angel."

Chapter Five
THE BIG SPLURGE

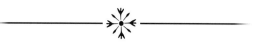

After years of traveling in the van with the bike and loaded suitcases, we began seriously considering purchasing a motorhome. Previously, Tammy had traveled extensively in a Dutch Star motorhome with Larry, tackling his bucket list while living with cancer. Though Bob had no experience with motorhomes, he always harbored the thought of eventually driving a semi-truck. When Bob mentioned this to Tammy, she could hardly contain herself. She immediately shouted, "Well then, you would love driving an RV!"

The discussion continued regarding the benefits of owning a motorhome. We could travel with our Shih Tzu, Zoey. Tammy would be confident of the cleanliness of our environment, unlike some hotels. In Bob's approaching retirement years, we could use it to travel and spend our winters in the south, far away from the cold Midwest. We could also use it to visit family in other states, travel with grandkids, and complete our fifty-state bicycling goal.

We researched the benefits of owning a fifth wheel versus a motorhome and the pros and cons of diesel engines compared to gasoline engines. We looked at a few used motorhomes and had taken one for a test drive, but it didn't pass our inspection.

While relaxing in our comfy home watching television one evening, we saw an ad for an upcoming RV show to be held at the Peoria Civic Center. We marked it on our calendar. We were excited to see different makes and models and talk with people who knew more about them than we did.

With no intention to buy anything, we enjoyed touring the beautiful displays. We commented on layouts, flooring, slides, amenities, and colors. We toured toy haulers and liked the idea of hauling our tandem in the back, but we thought motorhomes were stronger and safer. We had planned to eventually buy a diesel motorhome, possibly in a year or two, until we stepped into a 32-foot-long Winnebago Sunstar. The layout was the first thing that grabbed our attention. It had a king size bed, wooden drawers and closets, roomy storage, and a motorized bunk bed that lowered from the ceiling over the driver and passenger seat. Including the kitchen booth bed, bunk bed, and couch, we could accommodate three to four grandchildren. This seemed to be exactly what we had envisioned, but it had a gasoline engine, and we had been planning to buy a diesel rig.

When we entered the RV, we met another couple who seemed knowledgeable about motorhomes. They sensed our approval of the layout but noticed our ambivalence about purchasing a gasoline coach. Noticing our excitement and reluctance, the friendly couple was eager to ease our concerns. They had initially owned a diesel but switched to a gasoline model and were very happy with the change. Gasoline engines cost less to purchase and are easier to service. Tammy recalled friends from her RVing experience that also traded in a diesel for a gasoline model.

The owner of US Adventure RV (now Camper's Inn) in Davenport, Iowa, answered all our questions, and much to our surprise we signed the deal. Bob did ask that he throw in the two nice aluminum camp chairs that were on display outside the unit, and he readily agreed; after all, he was closing a deal. Several months later, the service manager provided an orientation on driving and usage, and in May of 2017 we set out on our first road trip to visit family in El Paso, Texas, in Sunny, our new motor coach. We were excited about the RV experience and the adventures ahead. Our first bike trip in the RV included six states in the northwest and five national parks.

Chapter Six
MURPHY'S LAW

Murphy's Law says, "If anything can go wrong, it will." A lot of planning goes into bike trips. Tammy researched flat, paved trails in scenic locations. She mapped out the distance between the rides, planned for housing (hotel or campsites), and searched for additional recreational activities and sights to visit. Thorough planning and preparation, however, did not prevent unexpected obstacles and detours.

For instance, in Hannibal, Missouri, we downloaded a long list of bike trails in the city. We did not know how to access the trails, so we stopped at the visitor's center for more information. They were surprised with our question and even more concerned about how we received the misinformation off the Internet. They did direct us to Riverview Park, but they were not aware that steep hills are next to impossible on the tandem. We did a lot of walking instead of riding that day.

The view from MacNally's, Ocracoke Island

In the North Carolina Outer Banks, Ocracoke Island was a suggested bike friendly island. The Hatteras Ferry took the van (with bicycle inside) and us to the island. We anticipated a great day of riding on the secluded getaway; however, the only decent trail we found, was adjacent to the road, and not very scenic. On top of that, it rained most of the time we were on Ocracoke. We were soaked to the skin at the end of our ride. Fortunately, tasty sandwiches at MacNally's, a quaint little restaurant overlooking the bay, helped salvage the day.

Biking in bear country

Another surprise occurred at Glacier National Park in Montana. The website described a scenic trail with a cascading waterfall. After we entered the park, we asked the ranger for directions to the trail. We parked in the lot per her instruction. The trail was very scenic with the tallest pines we have ever seen. But to our surprise, it was a very short trail used to link two adjacent areas of the park. So, we took the time to stop at another ranger station.

This time we were directed to a campground within the park. We rode on the main road, mostly a downhill descent, to the campground where we could supposedly access the trail. Upon our arrival, we spoke to a third ranger, who said, "There is no trail here." Now we were faced with the dreaded task of biking uphill to backtrack. Knowing that dusk was soon approaching, the ranger suggested a shortcut through the woods. Did she not know we were in bear country? Our options were riding the bike on a shorter, narrow trail through the dense woods or walking our bike up steep hills on the road. Neither sounded good to Tammy so she pawned the decision off on Bob.

Tammy was surprised that Bob chose the woods. She didn't question his decision, but in her mind, she thought it would be safer to travel the road rather than traverse through bear territory. Bob's rationale was that the shortcut was much faster, and sundown was rapidly approaching. Tammy carried the bear spray while Bob pushed the bike on the narrow trail and sang loudly, as Tammy insisted, to warn any bears of our approach! One never wants to surprise a bear. Tammy isn't afraid of very many things, but germs, alligators, sharks, and bears are on her short list.

There are many advantages to having an RV, but the more complex the operation, the more likely it is that something will go wrong. On a rather short trip to Arkansas, Louisiana, and Mississippi, we encountered more than our share of difficulties. Arriving at the KOA in Arkansas, a greeter escorted us to our lot and pointed to the bottom of our motorhome. The power assist rod was dangling about an inch from the ground. It should have been a foot off the ground! Bob asked me (Tammy) to step out of the motorhome to see the problem, and on the way out the door, one of us accidentally hit the red button, which automatically locked the door. Unfortunately, both sets of our keys were inside the motorhome. So now we were locked out with no keys or cell phones but with plenty of mosquitoes. Fortunately, Tammy had grabbed Zoey on the way out the door.

There is a real sense of community among campers. A friendly camper in the lot across from us came to our aid by loaning us his cell phone and giving us lemonade to drink. To get us out of our dilemma, the KOA office recommended we call I-55 Towing. The mechanic arrived within thirty minutes dressed in a blue uniform with fluorescent stripes. He used a wedge and a soft, inflatable bladder to crack the door open enough to insert a long metal rod with a hook on the end. After several attempts the door opened. He returned to our campsite at 9:30 am the following morning, screws and bolts in hand, to remount the steering assist rod. We were so relieved to be back on the road again! He was well paid for his time, but we still gave him a tip and several slices of homemade zucchini bread.

Setting up camp in North Little Rock, Arkansas

We drove two hours to the Downtown Riverside RV Park where we looked forward to not unhooking our tow dolly because we could access the Arkansas River Trail directly from our campsite. We worked together to set up camp hooking up all the mechanicals. By this point in our travels, we were able to do it in about fifteen minutes. Bob connects the outside electrical, plumbing, and sewer lines while Tammy has the more enjoyable tasks of pushing automatic leveling and power slide buttons inside.

The tandem bike is stored in our Dodge Caravan that we haul on the tow dolly. Additionally, it takes about fifteen minutes to unload and set up the bike. The rear seat needs to be reattached and Bob adjusts the seats and the handlebars to the appropriate positions.

We set out for a twenty-mile ride, and at the one-mile mark heard a loud pop. We thought it would be the inner tube but to our surprise realized we had punctured the back tire as well. We had spare tubes with us, but Bob had left the spare tire hanging on the wall in our garage. Because the bicycle shops were already closed, we went to Walmart and Academy Sports in North Little Rock and searched for a new tire. Unfortunately, neither store carried the appropriate size. On the road again, traveling to Louisiana, Tammy called six bicycle shops. Some did not have the appropriate size tire and other stores were closing soon and would not reopen until after Labor Day.

Capital Cyclery in Baton Rouge had the correct size but would not be open until Tuesday morning. We had two nights reserved at the French Quarter RV Resort in New Orleans. It was a very nice park, within four blocks of the French Quarter.

Since all bicycle shops were closed on Labor Day in New Orleans and in Baton Rouge, we went on a bayou alligator hunt with Cajun Pride Swamp Tours. Boating the scenic bayou, searching for alligators, and listening to Captain Danny's swamp stories distracted us from worrying about the bike.

The next morning Bob drove seventy-five miles back to Baton Rouge. The helpful staff at the bike shop offered several tire options while other stores didn't have any at all. By the time Bob returned from Baton Rouge, Tammy had uploaded, and edited pictures and video footage for three hours straight.

We postponed the ride until late afternoon since it was 98 degrees with about 90 percent humidity, but we did get in a fifteen-mile ride on the Tammany Trace Trail. We would have ridden further, but the foghorn on the bayou bridge warned us the gate to the bridge and the trail itself were closing. What a mess it would have been to be stranded on the wrong side of the bridge several miles from the van!

After two nights in Louisiana, we moved on to Mississippi. Again, due to the heat, we decided we would ride in the late afternoon and instead go to Biloxi Beach in the morning. As Bob slowed down for a stoplight on the Louisiana 90 Coastal Drive, a man on the curb gestured wildly at him to stop. Bob pulled over, got out, and saw what the man was so excited about. The right dolly tire was flat, and the rim was mangled. Bob made some quick phone calls and connected with E & M Towing. They were able to tow the dolly to A.W. Cook, a salvage and motor parts store. They tried to be helpful but unfortunately did not have the right size rim. An employee of A.W. Cook was just going off his shift. He volunteered to help Bob solve the tire and rim problem on his own time. He and Bob drove to two stores and called four others while Tammy and Zoey waited in the hot RV, not wanting to turn on the air conditioning since we were low on gas. Though hot, at least they had a nice view of the ocean.

At the seventh store, ten minutes before closing, the two men discovered Southern Tire Mart had the right size rim and tire. They rushed to the store and $95.41 later had a tire and rim in hand. The miracle mechanic took Bob back to the salvage yard to install it on the tow dolly. Four hours after the incident, he towed the trailer back to the RV in Biloxi. When the mechanic brought it back, he noticed the Blue Ox power assist rod hanging near the ground. He removed the damaged rod, and we drove the remainder of the trip without it. When we asked what we owed him for his time and expertise he responded, "It's up to you. I like helping people." Bob and I agreed to give him our $200 spare cash. Ecstatic, he gave Tammy and Bob an unwanted, big greasy hug.

Due to the tire debacle, biking the Longleaf Trace Trail in Mississippi was delayed until the following morning. At 9:00 pm, we finally arrived at the Okatoma RV Resort, which we had difficulty finding in the dark. It was located ten miles in the country outside of Hattiesburg. We hooked up, went directly to sleep, planning an early morning ride since we needed to unhook and check out before 11:00 am. At sunrise, we rode 25 miles on the flat, paved trail lined on both sides with well-marked beautiful southern trees. We got back to camp, showered, and were off for what we hoped would be an uneventful day.

We still needed to bike in Arkansas, which was on our itinerary for this three-state trip, so, after biking in Mississippi, we headed back towards North Little Rock. While driving through Monticello, Arkansas, Bob heard a sickening sound. It reminded him of the sound he had heard in Biloxi. This time he recognized it and immediately pulled over into a large Burger King parking lot. To our dismay, the new tire was completely shredded. Fortunately, the rim was not seriously damaged. Customers at Burger King tried to help, but Bob was already on the phone with the owner of Tire Town, the only tire store still open at 6:45 pm. The owner and his assistant arrived within fifteen minutes. They jacked up the dolly, removed the damaged tire, and drove the rim back to their shop to install a used tire that was just the right size. Within half an hour, we were amazed to be back on the road again.

Leary of damaging a tire on the dolly again, Tammy drove behind the motorhome in the Dodge Caravan. We arrived at the Downtown Riverside RV Park in North Little Rock at 9:00 pm and were biking by seven o'clock the next morning. The Arkansas River Trail was rated as one of the top Southern Bike Trails in the nation in 2011, and we could see why. On our twenty-mile ride, we discussed whether to hook the van back on the tow dolly for the return home. Tammy had not slept well, so Bob made the decision to load the van on the dolly and hope for the best. After an uneventful day on the road, we arrived home at 9:00 pm.

In April of 2020 we had planned a two-week motorhome/bike trip in Florida with stops in Kentucky, Tennessee, and Alabama. But in March the Coronavirus pandemic changed everything. Like most people in the US, we were on lockdown in our home. All elective, non-essential travel was forbidden. Tammy canceled RV Park reservations while Bob prepared to conduct virtual office visits with his neurology patients via telephone or Zoom, a web-based conferencing site. Wearing required face masks, we grocery shopped every other week, trying to remain calm about the situation. Some goods quickly became scarce including toilet paper, hand sanitizer, and peanut butter.

On March 22, 2020, CNN reported 26,000 cases in the US and 308,000 worldwide. There had been 13,049 deaths worldwide and 316 deaths in the US. Italy alone had 5,000 deaths at that point. New York Governor Andrew Cuomo said, "Life will knock you on your butt. This is a period of challenge for this generation."

In just two months, by May 20, the current deaths were over 90,000 with 1,518,661 cases in the United States. The pandemic hit home with us. Tammy's sister-in-law tested positive for Covid-19. She was quarantined at home with her family for fourteen days. Fortunately, she made a good recovery, and no one else in the household became ill. By Memorial Day weekend, all 50 states began to re-open with restrictions in place. We rescheduled our trip for later in the summer although concerned about Florida heat in July.

Biking in the horse capital of the world

On the southern trip, we enjoyed a beautiful bike ride in the horse capital of the United States, Georgetown, Kentucky, visited with family in Tennessee, and then headed down to Florida. We stopped at Denny's, one of our favorite restaurants, in Goodhope, Alabama. Back on the road, Bob could not avoid hitting a "gator." This was not an alligator but a large throw-off from a retread semi-truck tire. We pulled over to a rest stop for Bob to examine the undercarriage. He could tell that the tail pipe had been somewhat flattened but since the RV seemed to be running well, we decided to continue on, planning to get a full assessment in Florida.

When we stopped for gas about an hour further down the road, Bob discovered he no longer had his wallet. Bob called to verify the whereabouts of the wallet at Denny's in Goodhope, and once confirmed, we decided to go back to pick it up. Despite two and a half hours of unnecessary delay, we still made it to Pensacola Beach by late afternoon.

In the morning we contacted the head of parts and service at US Adventure RV in Davenport, Iowa, where we purchased our RV. He suggested we have it inspected immediately because a damaged exhaust system could destroy our engine. After making several phone calls, Bob finally reached a local RV tech repairman who agreed to look at the rig onsite. He cut off three feet of the flattened exhaust and was able to open the system enough for us to continue our journey. He was most concerned though with the thick, goopy, black coating that covered the underside. He suggested we have the brakes and ball joints inspected. The mechanics at Pep Boys did a thorough inspection and assured us that nothing was wrong. When we discussed this with US Adventure RV, they informed us the "goop" was the protective coating we have applied once a year to make our rig mouse-proof. The local mechanic who had the goop all over his arms said, "Don't get that done anymore."

Chapter Seven
CONVERSATIONS

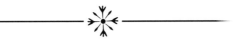

One advantage of the tandem is that we can talk with each other as we ride. When two people are riding individual bikes it is not always easy to talk, and because neither of us has great hearing, the tandem was a good solution. Some of our best conversations have occurred on the trails. Discussions have been all over the map, including family, retirement, traveling, spiritual things, and changes in our aging bodies.

Events in our lives have long-lasting effects. Due to the untimely deaths of Larry and Barb, our former spouses, we have had deep conversations about our eventual deaths. Funeral planning is a taboo subject with most people, but not with us. On one bike trip, Tammy said to Bob, "I think I'll die before you, but if not, I need to know whom you would like to speak at your funeral."

"Family members," Bob replied.

"But your career is a big part of your story," Tammy said.

"I have been a neurologist for years. I don't mind you talking a little about my career, and perhaps one representative from Carle could speak; however, my faith, my family, and my friends are what really matter," Bob responded.

Tammy received bereavement training and served as a hospice volunteer working with grieving families. She encouraged patients to be proactive in making funeral arrangements and helped several families create memorial DVDs. She understood how difficult and draining it could be to plan a funeral on short notice. Bob promised Tammy he would write out his obituary and funeral wishes, and he indeed followed through with his promise. Song choices and many details were listed, including having a pizza party and ice cream celebration. With Tammy's strong interest and expertise in photography and videography, she will have plenty of material for memorable DVDs for Bob and herself.

We have talked in detail about our former lives. Marrying another person who had experienced the painful death of a spouse facilitated open communication. Initially in our marriage, we both talked frequently about the pain of our losses. We spoke about the initial diagnoses, the journey through illness, and the difficult final days.

Not being with Larry during his final moments, as he had wished, was a recurring pain for Tammy. She was with him continuously as his caretaker for months prior to his death. Sadly, the actual moment of his passing occurred when he had stepped into another room.

For Bob, a painful aspect of Barb's experience was the extreme fatigue during the twenty-one months from the time of her diagnosis to her death. Five different courses of chemotherapy, multiple hospitalizations and surgeries, coupled with her desire to continue teaching as long as she could, left her with almost no energy for meaningful social interaction. As we opened up about that area of loss, it naturally led to other discussions about difficult times in our lives.

We were transparent. Heartaches and difficulties from our past were shared. Tammy was open about growing up without her father, who died when she was only four and a half and the pain of going through a divorce. The death of a family member is final, but the death of a family unit is an ongoing pain.

At the time of the divorce, Tammy was diagnosed with Stage II Melanoma. Despite a resection with clean margins, the fear of a recurrence never left her mind. During this time, she also was being evaluated for an autoimmune disorder. After several years this was eventually diagnosed as Mixed Connective Tissue Disease (MCTD). Tammy always felt that the stresses she had endured in her past brought on the melanoma and the MCTD.

Bob shared about the mixed blessings of growing up as a missionary kid in the Philippines. There were many interesting sights, sounds, foods, and experiences. It was fun being immersed in another culture, but he always felt like an outsider, even when he returned to the United States to attend college.

Bob said, "When I was applying to medical school, statistics showed that for every accepted student, two other equally qualified students were rejected." Despite solid MCAT scores and a high grade point average, Bob was not accepted the first year he applied. When he was accepted the following year, he entered the four most academically rigorous years of his education.

More than half of all doctors face at least one malpractice suit in their career. Besides the death of Barb and his parents, the worst experience Bob had was when, early in his career, he was named in a medical malpractice suit. He was eventually exonerated; however, Bob reveals, "The pain never really goes away."

We have also discussed past travels. Both of us had traveled extensively in the United States and elsewhere, but we still looked forward to biking and exploring all fifty states as a couple.

Our adult children and their families are frequently on our minds. With some parents, when their children are out of sight, they are out of mind. With us, the proverb that dates to the 1500s does not apply. We relish their personal victories but hurt with them when they experience difficulties or loss. We love hearing from them and being in the loop about their thoughts, plans, and experiences.

Rader Family Farm, Normal, Illinois

At any given time, one of the grandkids pops into our minds. We smile, and often laugh, as we discuss enjoyable times we have had with them: swimming, biking, reading, camping, and teaching them new games like Skip-Bo, a Cranston favorite. For five years in a row, when we lived in Bloomington, Illinois, we took the grandkids to Rader Family Farms, a fourth generation working farm. The family has come up with unique ways to reinvent common agriculture related items to use in their attractions. Unlike other fall-themed venues, this family run farm plays Christian music and does not cater to the dark themes prevalent at other facilities.

The grandchildren have reignited our own sense of wonder as we look at the world through their eyes. They give us a heightened sense of energy but remind our aging bodies that we are not as young as we used to be.

We are thankful that their parents FaceTime with us and send us clips of activities we would have otherwise missed. We cherish their unique personalities and character traits. Like many grandparents, we brag about their interests, creativity, musical skills, curiosity, and bravery. As they grow and develop, we encourage them to flourish with a sense of purpose. We consider our children and grandchildren our primary mission field.

Chapter Eight
WE ALL LOSE GROUND

——— ❄ ———

Our past has created an acute awareness of how suddenly a physical challenge can arise or circumstances can change. Even before our marriage we were faced with the realization that Tammy, historically a coordinated acrobat and dancer, was having difficulty with her balance. She would frequently bump into Bob during their evening walks. Bob encouraged her to seek medical attention, which revealed a schwannoma of the eighth nerve. Also called "acoustic neuromas," these benign tumors, if left untreated, can cause paralysis, deafness, and even death. We were faced with the decision to proceed with skull-based surgery or gamma knife radiation therapy. Because Tammy was in college, and a newlywed, she opted for the gamma knife treatment at Barnes Jewish Hospital in St. Louis.

The radiation resulted in leaving Tammy deaf in her left ear. As a result of aging, Bob has lost some hearing in the high frequency ranges. This is one reason the tandem works so much better than riding two separate bikes. We ride to preserve our cardiovascular fitness, and it is a less painful form of exercise given our arthritic knees! We aim to stay as healthy as possible as long as we can.

Over the ten years we have biked to maintain our fitness, we have realized we are losing ground. Our joints hurt more, it is harder to get up off the ground, and our stamina is not what it used to be. And like many other adults our age, when nature calls, we must respond much more quickly than when we were younger. Available bathrooms have become welcome sights.

Flare-ups of Tammy's MCTD can cause her to experience significant fatigue. Not getting proper sleep compounds this. At this stage in our life, we make allowances for our physical limitations. We plan shorter driving days on the road with the motorhome. We now try to limit our driving to no more than five to six hours. We attempt to bike early before the heat of the day and before the energy slump we often experience in the afternoon.

We had begun to seriously consider where we might like to retire. Considering our health concerns, we both liked the idea of retiring to a warm climate with accessible biking and walking trails. On our rescheduled bike trip to Florida in July of 2020, we enjoyed riding on the flat, paved, scenic trail in Pensacola Beach on Santa Rosa Island. While we were on the route, Tammy recognized a beautiful, resort condominium complex that she had noticed twelve years previous when traveling with Larry, Portofino Island Resort.

Because the bike trail went directly in front of the resort, we decided to stop and ask for a tour of the facility. Kelly Sakey, realtor for the condo towers, was more than willing to show us the breathtaking views in an available two-bedroom unit. It didn't take us long to recognize the benefits of living in an environment like this where we could swim, bike, or walk anytime we wanted. With an indoor Olympic-size pool, we could swim inside during the cooler months and ride our bike almost any day of the year. And the balcony view, in and of itself, is very therapeutic. We began considering retirement in Florida.

The next stop on our bicycle tour was Gulf Shores, Alabama. We had previously ridden our bike on the Chief Ladiga Trail, in northern Alabama, but we looked forward to biking on the Hugh Branyon Backcountry Trail at Gulf Shores State Park, just an hour west of Pensacola. After a scenic, tiring 31-mile ride and a short visit to Orange Beach, we noticed an open house sign at a condominium. We thought it would be useful to explore options in Orange Beach and compare them with those in Pensacola Beach, so we stopped to tour the facility. There we met a REMAX realtor and arranged to visit properties the following day. In five hours, we toured six condos.

We received preliminary information from Kelly, and on our return trip to Illinois, we called numerous times to ask questions and obtain further information about Portofino. We were surprised to be considering selling the beautiful home that we built for ourselves in Bloomington, Illinois, in proximity to family. But as our family had grown and dispersed, this presented an opportunity to spread our wings in an area that would be beneficial for our health and allow us to travel in the RV to see family.

As much as we loved the long bike trail system in Alabama, there was no comparison with the gem we discovered in Portofino. In Orange Beach, the beaches were packed with many tourists, whereas Santa Rosa Island is less commercialized with miles of national protected seashores. While it is clearly a matter of taste, the serenity of Pensacola Beach was a better fit for us.

Chapter Nine
A GOOD FIT

In the summer of 2020, Bob celebrated his 65th birthday. The following July culminated thirty years of continuous work at Carle Foundation Hospital. To Bob, thirty years seemed like a benchmark for a sense of completion. Due to our aging bodies, our dispersing families, and the milestone of thirty years working at Carle, we decided to officially retire in July of 2021.

We had originally planned to maintain our home in Bloomington and travel south to various warmer locations during the winter. However, several factors made us change our plans. Recent deaths in the family heightened our sense of loss. In passing, Bob said, "Everywhere we go reminds us of our losses." Bob's approaching retirement, and the inevitable changes in relationships to Carle and Champaign-Urbana, would be another significant loss.

National Seashore on Santa Rosa Island

In our travels throughout the United States, we have noticed beauty everywhere. However, we are drawn to warmer weather, the ocean, and unspoiled natural beauty. While Oregon fits this description, the water is much colder than the Gulf, and it is too far from friends and family. The desert states have the warmth, but not the water. The natural beauty of Santa Rosa Island with grasses, dunes, and emerald green waters enchanted us. Half of the island is a protected national seashore, and no commercial or residential building can be constructed within the area. Consequently, the opportunity to enjoy wildlife such as birds, turtles, and sea life is ensured for the foreseeable future. While it seems a long way from Illinois, on several occasions, we have made the trip in a single, long day of driving.

Balcony view, Tower 5, 19th floor

Having made this decision to retire, we continued our conversation with Kelly Sakey. She supplied us with pictures and details of available listings at Portofino. We considered whether to buy a two-bedroom or three-bedroom unit, but with the hope of having friends and family visit, we settled on the three-bedroom option. Within three weeks of returning home from our bike trip, we flew back to tour an available three-bedroom condo on the 19th floor. The 480 sq. ft. balcony had amazing views of the sound, the island, and the Gulf. Our taste in interior design differed somewhat from the previous owner, which is often the case, but we decided to make an offer! In the next six weeks we finalized all the details and closed on the property at our bank in Illinois.

After being primary caretakers for three of our grandchildren for four and a half months in Illinois while their mother was deployed, we took a much-needed two-week vacation to our beach condo in Florida after Christmas. It was beneficial for us to replenish our energy and get a sense of what winter in northern Florida would be like. Most days, the weather was sunny, with an average temperature in the sixties. With Tammy's cold sensitivity, she spent most of the winter in Illinois indoors. Portofino was a delightful contrast to the ice, snow, and sub-freezing temperature of Bloomington. We swam in the indoor pool, biked, and walked every day. This was a foretaste of how this future home would be a good fit for our retirement years.

It's a challenge to know when to put your home on the market. We planned to list our home in the summer and move in the fall, but with low home lending rates and high housing demand we decided to list in the spring instead. To help defray mortgage payments, we signed a one-year rental agreement with Premier, an on-site property management agency, at Portofino Island Resort. Due to scheduled rental reservations over the busy summer season, we would not be able to move into the condo until September. Our plan, should the house sell quickly, would be to live in our RV until we could make the move. We scheduled the entire month of August to finish our endeavor to bike in all fifty states but decided to cancel the trip since our house hadn't sold. We needed to downsize to prepare for the move, so that summer we sold or donated roughly half of our belongings. This was amazingly freeing.

In mid-September, we drove Sunny and pulled the van so we could leave the motorhome at Move It Storage, an RV storage facility we secured in Navarre, Florida. We painted most of the walls in our condo before returning home in the van. In October, we rented an eighteen-foot U-Haul, which our nephew helped load. Sarah and Tristan, another niece and nephew, met us in Florida to help us unload in exchange for taking some of the previous homeowners' furniture. Tristan is strong and handy and worked above and beyond what we had hoped for. He hooked up our sound system and installed several light fixtures. Sarah was helpful in giving decorating advice. We look forward to their family visiting in the future when we can focus on fun activities rather than work.

Blue Angel Chips with bleu cheese

Three weeks after our move, we were settled enough to have Tammy's sister, Nila, visit for a week to celebrate Tammy's sixtieth birthday. We enjoyed beach time, jigsaw puzzles, Skip-Bo, swimming, and a speed boat ride in Destin to see dolphins. We dined at several of our favorite locations on the island and chose The Grand Marlin for Tammy's birthday lunch. This restaurant caters to her vegetarian diet, and it offers a Blue Angel Chip appetizer with a homemade bleu cheese dressing that is to die for. On top of that, they have the best Key lime pie on the island.

We were praying for our home in Illinois to sell before winter and in mid-November we received an offer. After several negotiations, we settled and closed on the property in December. We made another trip to Illinois, rented a ten-foot U-Haul trailer, cleaned out our remaining belongings and thoroughly cleaned the home. Our attorney handled the closing arrangements so that we would not have to return.

Unfortunately, just prior to our trip to Illinois, our twelfth grandchild, Tebel Robert Kern, was born prematurely and died soon after birth, in Berrien Springs, Michigan. It had been a difficult pregnancy for Amelia, and Tebel's death hit us all very hard. They had a beautiful memorial service in the seminary chapel on the grounds of Andrews University which Tyler attends. Tebel was buried in a basket, like baby Moses, in the children's section at Rose Hill Cemetery. Tyler, Amelia, and their four surviving children (Topher, Aurora, Treeland, and Tyson) were surrounded by family, friends, and a community of believers from their church, the Grace Place, and Andrews Seminary. At the gravesite we read and dropped the following letter in his burial plot:

Dear Tebel,

We are sad that we didn't get to meet you and hold you. You are special to us, our twelfth grandchild. Papa is touched that you bear his first name as your middle name. We will miss celebrating birthdays and holidays with you. More than that though, we will miss getting to know you, watching you grow, delighting in your unique personality, and seeing you become the man God intended you to be.

Grammy and Papa promise to comfort your family and keep your memory alive as we all struggle with your death. We look forward to the day in heaven when we get to hold you in our arms for the first time and it will not be the last. We long for the resurrection. What a glorious day that will be! Jesus loves you and so do we.

Love,
Grammy and Papa

This was our first Christmas alone, not surrounded by children or grandchildren. It was different, but we tried to make it good. In the past, we had big celebrations and sometimes attended cold, snowy city street parades or light festivals. What a change to watch and film a lighted boat parade on the bay at our new home. We are thankful for FaceTime which allowed us to not only talk but to see and interact with our children and grandchildren.

Walking the beach hand in hand

In December, we had two families visit. First, Joanna, with her son, Hunter, and two daughters, Lexi and Emmy, came a week prior to Christmas. Emmy was excited to see the ocean for the first time. It was too chilly for swimming, but the kids enjoyed making sandcastles and searching for seashells.

We learned that downtown Pensacola hosts "Winterfest," with activities catering to children during the Christmas season. Lexi, Hunter, and Emmy rode on a city trolley, Polar Express Ride, which was a little chilly at this time of year. When we arrived home, we made hot chocolate to warm them up before bedtime.

Timothy navigating the
Portofino trail.

Dan and Beth, the second family to visit in December, arrived for a week-long visit after Christmas with our grandson, Timothy. He loved riding his scooter on the trail and swimming. He specifically requested to visit an aquarium. At only five years old, his request surprised us. We realized we had a treasure in the Gulfarium, which is on Okaloosa Island, and we have taken many visitors there since.

We took both families to meet "Sweet Pea" at the Navarre Beach Sea Turtle Conservation Center. Sweet Pea, a rescued green sea turtle, will live out the rest of her life at the facility due to her fin amputation, shell damage, and internal injuries from a boat hit and fishing net entanglement. Since our island is a sea turtle hatching location, this center serves to educate and rehabilitate injured sea animals. We bought an annual membership, and we take all our visitors to meet Sweet Pea.

Kathy and Lindsey, friends from our Bloomington Church, came to visit during Lindsey's spring break from Illinois State University. We did many of the usual tourist activities, and especially enjoyed the dolphin cruise in Destin. On one occasion the three women had a special girls' day out and came home with new clothes and stories to tell. We look forward to having them return.

Turner and Talon sworn in as Junior Rangers

We were blessed to have Turner and Talon, the two oldest of our Illinois grandchildren, visit us for a three-day weekend. Thatcher is only two years-old and we hope to have him visit in the future with his father, Travis. Papa Bob flew to St. Louis to pick up the boys and returned with them the same day. We packed a lot in three days–swimming, beach time, meeting Sweet Pea, biking, and visiting the Gulfarium. The boys were entertained by the dolphin and sea lion shows. They were the first grandkids to complete and earn their Gulf Islands National Seashore Junior Ranger badges. They learned how to be aware of the flag colors (red, double red, green, yellow, purple) for beach safety, among other things.

Family bike train

Tyler's family was originally scheduled to visit in December, but with the circumstances and his busy schedule, the visit was postponed until his spring break at the end of March. Besides enjoying the beach and swimming, we rented a pontoon boat with a slide. Since this was so early in the spring, the sea was cooler than we would have liked. Regardless, all the children braved the cold water and went down the slide. In the spring, the bayside inflatable obstacle course opened. Papa, Tyler, Amelia, and the kids were challenged by the balance beams, trampoline, climbing hills, and swing. Grammy remained ashore to photograph the fun. And, as usual, we made sure we got in a bike trip with the grandkids!

In the short time we have been here, these visits from family and friends have helped make the transition to our new home enjoyable. We are thankful we chose a location that is enticing and has a lot to offer. It's a good fit for us as a couple as well as for our extended family and friends.

Chapter Ten
THE FINAL SEVEN

After nine years of extensive travel, we planned a one-month trip to finish our goal to bike in all fifty states. This final trip included seven states–Texas, New Mexico, Arizona, Nevada, Utah, Oklahoma, and Kansas. We also planned to visit White Sands National Park, Zion National Park, and Arches National Park.

One of thousands of 'gators on Pintail Wildlife Drive

Now that we live in Florida, we charted a southern route and stopped in Louisiana at the Lake Charles East/Iowa KOA Journey RV Park. The following day we explored the Creole Nature Trail, one of Louisiana's National Scenic Byways. We stopped at Pintail Wildlife Drive and Boardwalk for Tammy to photograph birds with her new Nikon telephoto lens. On the loop, there were warning signs not to get out of one's car due to the estimated 15,000 alligators that call this place home. We heeded this prohibition and nonetheless were able to capture outstanding photos from inside our vehicle.

We also stayed at a KOA Campground in San Antonio, Texas. KOAs are our first choice due to their service, cleanliness, and catering to children and pets. We planned to bike on the San Antonio River Walk and Bike Path, but once we hooked up our coach at the KOA, we noticed a nice, paved trail immediately adjacent to the campsite. This was an unexpected find that made it convenient to get in our twenty miles without having to transport the bike.

The following morning, we visited the San Antonio Botanical Garden, hiked the River Walk, and had lunch at Saltgrass Restaurant, overlooking the water. The bridges, architecture, and landscaping were impressive on this historical landmark. Total distance walked for the day was over seven miles.

Picturesque sunset at White Sands National Park

Our next stop was Alamogordo, New Mexico. We got the oil changed in both vehicles and as dusk approached, we drove the van to White Sands National Park for sunset photos. With childlike enthusiasm, we sledded down gypsum hills, made snow angels in the sand, and jumped and climbed the sandy slopes. The next day we returned for an early morning, thirty-mile bike ride. We beat the heat and crowds and were able to obtain good photos and video.

As retirees we decided to slow down with the drive time but not the activities. For this trip, we stayed in each location for two to three days. We planned to visit four national parks but also allowed ourselves some free time to venture out and explore. With a free afternoon, Tammy contacted a friend who had previously lived in Alamogordo and asked her for hiking suggestions.

Her friend suggested the Osha Trail in Cloudcroft, a part of the Lincoln National Forrest. Tired from biking, we hoped for no more than a two-mile hike in the mountains. Unfortunately, due to poor signage, our endeavor turned into a four-mile hike. Just under a year previous, Tammy had undergone surgery on her left foot for plantar fasciitis. She experienced a long recovery and did not want to incur a setback. The difficult terrain reminded us of our ordeal on the Koko Crater Trail in Hawaii.

On finishing the hike, tired and hungry, we longed for a hearty meal. We drove into the picturesque mountain town of Cloudcroft. With its quaint restaurants, country stores, and wooden boardwalks, Tammy said, "This town is a perfect site for a Hallmark movie."

Dave's Café, complete with live mountain music, offered several vegetarian options and was a delight for Tammy. She seldom has the luxury of having several options, if any. Bob's only disappointment was that the ice cream stand inside the restaurant had closed an hour earlier. On our way out of town, we had our first sighting of wild elk.

Passing through southern New Mexico en route to see family in Tucson, Arizona, we encountered our first sandstorm. While we didn't have to stop, we did have to slow down to about thirty miles per hour. After the long drive, the Tucson/Lazydays KOA Resort was a welcome retreat. Aside from the West Glacier KOA Resort, this was our second-favorite KOA so far.

One of the main reasons we came through Tucson was to connect with the Bauer Family. Aunt Mary, who advised us at our wedding to always have our camera ready because she loved Tammy's pictures, met us at The Locale Italian Restaurant with her son, John, and daughter and son-in-law, Tina and Dave Starck. Because it was our tenth anniversary and we were close to reaching our biking goal, they gifted us with a metal tandem bike statuette which we decided to keep in our RV. The food and conversation were great. Afterwards, we went to Steve and Maria Sara Bauer's house for dessert and freshly squeezed juice from their home-grown grapefruit trees.

The Saguaro National Park sign we saw on our way into town nudged us into adding this park to our itinerary list. The scenic drive included the largest number of saguaro cacti in one location in the United States. We took lots of pictures and even took a short hike.

Although we make biking plans with extensive research, we always remain open to new possibilities. So, when Dave Starck offered to ride with us on the Tucson Loop Trail, accessible from his home, we readily agreed. This was the first time we had a companion and guide on a twenty-mile ride.

On the way to the Grand Canyon, we stayed at Apache Junction KOA to visit with Dennis and Mary Henry, Barb's oldest sister and husband. We also planned to visit Ruth Finger, Barb's mother, who just celebrated her 100th birthday in April. But due to Covid and low staffing at her assisted living home this was not possible.

Keeping our distance while watching the horses

A tip from a photographer we met, routed us to Coons Bluff Recreation Area to capture photos of wild horses. We were astonished to walk openly on wooded acres near the Salt River. We probably hiked about forty-five minutes before another hiker confirmed their location. Trekking forward, we soon came across a herd. As we stayed and shot pictures and video, two other herds approached and walked through the area. Many of them were not very active, ready to rest for the evening, but we were able to witness two stallions seemingly seeking to establish dominance. These unplanned outings often make the trips so memorable.

Originally, we had planned to bike at the Grand Canyon, but since we had biked in Tucson, we now had more time to explore the beauty of this national park in other ways. We were aware that people book activities, such as mule rides, a year in advance, but we decided to take our chance. We called Xanterra Canyon Vista Mule Ride, and they asked how many were in our party. As expected, we were put on a waiting list. We were pleasantly surprised to receive a call the following morning. We were bumped up on the waiting list because there were only two in our party, and they could not accommodate some of the larger group requests.

At the lodge we were weighed and signed our releases. At 9:00 the next morning we hit the trail on Algebra (Tammy's mule) and Lucy (Bob's mule). Our guides led our group on a scenic ride along the South

Rim. These mules were veterans, skillfully navigating the rocky terrain. We were just along for the ride! In addition to photos, we took video with our GoPro.

On the mule ride we recorded each other, but one unique aspect of our GoPro footage is to record us as a couple hiking and biking together. While walking or biking, we keep our eyes open for tree limbs, posts, or any stable objects to clip the GoPro on. After editing, we upload short movies of our journeys on Facebook for our followers, who often ask, "Who is taking your video?" or "How do you get both of you in the shots?" After attaching the GoPro, one of us runs back to the other person to record both of us in the scenic shots. It's a lot of work, but well worth the effort.

View at South Rim, Grand Canyon

Tammy has videos of biking trips and vacations, and she has also begun adding clips of our hiking in national parks to her collection. On our last evening in the canyon, we decided to hike the South Rim Trail. We wanted to record a beautiful shot of us walking around a curve with the canyon highlighted in the background. Finding a strong, high limb, Bob reached to attach the GoPro. He leveled it, pushed record, and as he stepped down, he lost his footing on uneven rocks. Taking a hard fall, he landed on his left hand and face. Fortunately, no bones were broken, but he did have a bruise and gash on his left cheek visible for many days and a jammed index finger that will probably never heal.

Hike at Zion National Park

The next national park on our route was Zion National Park. Due to our limited time, we chose to spend our day touring by using the hop on/off propane-powered shuttle in order to see as many highlights as possible. The convenient bus serves to limit auto congestion and pollution in the park. We hiked several trails with majestic views and spotted lots of wild turkeys.

We signed up for an early morning Utility Terrain Vehicle (UTV) ride with East Zion Adventures. On the off-road guided tour, we explored two different slot canyons. The lighting inside was remarkable but getting through the canyon was often challenging with rocks, narrow openings, and tree limbs.

On our drive to the excursion, we realized Bryce Canyon National Park was only an hour past Orderville, the location of our adventure. While this park was not on our list to tour, we had previously discussed visiting all 63 national parks as our next travel goal. Immediately after touring the slot canyons, we decided to go for it, and we were glad we did!

Bryce Canyon National Park

The hoodoos, pillars of rock up to 150 feet high, make an unusual landscape. Bryce Canyon reportedly has the largest concentration of hoodoos in the world. The scenery reminded us of our trip to Cappadocia, Turkey. With only a few hours to tour, the park ranger recommended we hike Sunrise Point and Sunset Point. We also descended the steep mountain trail a short distance towards Queens Garden.

En route to Moab, where we planned to do our Utah biking, we spontaneously decided, once again, to make a short detour to Capitol Reef National Park. In the RV, and having Zoey with us, we toured the farmstead where we enjoyed delicious pie with homegrown cherries and ended our visit by viewing ancient petroglyphs.

Arriving late at Portal RV Resort in Moab, Utah, we unhooked our tow dolly. The pull-through site we had originally booked in October was no longer available. Because we wanted to access the Moab Canyon Bike Path directly from the RV resort, we settled for a less convenient back-in campsite.

"The Windows" at Arches National Park

Of the five national parks in Utah, Arches National Park was the only location that required an entrance reservation. With the hope of watching a sunrise on the red rock mountains, we entered the park at 6:45 am. In awe, we stopped to photograph unique formations such as the Three Gossips, Balanced Rock, and Skyline Arch. We came across a professional photographer at "The Windows" and agreed to photograph each other.

The iconic Delicate Arch, pictured on the Utah license plate, was a "must see" on our schedule. It may be our age, but the 3.5-mile round trip hike on rocky terrain up a mountain and around cliffs was grueling. We stood in line with another couple who had a DSLR camera and photographed each other as we stood under the massive arch.

Tired, we pushed ourselves to hike another two miles at Devils Garden to see Landscape Arch. The red cliff walls, blue skies, and fluffy white clouds visible along the path and through the arch were stunning. In the future, we would like to hike further on this trail to view other arches.

After a light lunch in the RV and a short rest, we ventured out on the bike route. We came across a Dutch couple who offered to take our photo as we began to set up our photography gear. Because of them, we now have one of only three photos of the two of us biking together. We talked with this friendly couple for a while about our fifty-state biking goal and their US touring plans. A twenty-mile bike ride and seven miles of hiking at Arches National Park made for sore feet and a good night's sleep.

Portal Jeep Tour, Sand Flats Recreation Area

The following morning the adventures continued but without any physical exertion. Months earlier we had reserved a Portal Jeep Tour offered by the resort. This tour involves serious off-road adventure, climbing over rocks in the Sand Flats Recreation. Our tour guide drove our electric blue Rubicon Jeep up steep rocky mountains on the Hell's Revenge Trail. We are always open to new adventures, and this excursion did not disappoint!

On our last afternoon in Moab, we visited Canyonlands National Park. We stopped at the visitor center, got our national parks book stamped, and mapped out our plans with a park ranger. Shafer Canyon, an unexpected stop, was our favorite for several reasons. The layered colors in the background and the large, flat plateau beckoned us to walk out on it. At the end of the plateau, we discovered a short but narrow hiking path along the canyon wall, which we ventured out on as well. In Utah, our forty-eighth state to bike, we had planned to visit three national parks but were delighted to tour all five.

Our last two states of the final seven were Oklahoma and Kansas. We rode twenty miles in each state on nice trails that were not overly scenic. In Kansas, our fiftieth state, we were tired and had to push ourselves to complete our ten-year project. There was a sense of gratification but also a sense of letdown. We have been working on this project for a decade, from 2013 to 2022, and we had successfully accomplished our goal. It was reminiscent of our dating years when emotions fluctuated between holding on and letting go.

Chapter Eleven
SIGHTS AND SOUNDS

Portland Head Light, most photographed lighthouse in the USA

In our quest to ride in all fifty states, we visited twenty-one national parks, took pictures of twenty-five lighthouses, visited several national sites, hiked valleys and mountains, and reconnected with family members. The sights and sounds were amazing. Every location was unique and had something to offer, but there were certain places and priceless memories that will be forever etched in our minds.

Sharing a country road in Kalona, Iowa

In Indiana, we heard bubbling creeks and the sound of rattling wooden planks as we biked over covered bridges. In Kalona, Iowa, we watched an Amish man drive his horse-drawn buggy down a country road. This inspired us to explore the Amish farms and stores in that community where we later biked.

Our Midwest bike trip to Wisconsin, Minnesota, Iowa, and Missouri took place before we purchased the motorhome. Hotel arrangements were made in every state except for Wisconsin, our neighboring state. Our first ride was in Madison. We were not sure if we would spend the night there but anticipated no problem in finding a hotel in such a large city. Unbeknownst to us, there was a multi-state softball tournament taking place in Madison that weekend. All hotels had "no vacancy" in Madison, and when we inquired at hotels for the next three hours while driving towards Minneapolis, they too were full.

Finally, at 11:45 pm Bob prayed, "Dear God, please find us a hotel before midnight." We were watching for vacancy signs, and when the next hotel in sight did not have a sign, regardless, we decided to stop and check for availability. Bob approached the reception desk at the Best Western Hotel in Falls River, Wisconsin and inquired, "You wouldn't have any vacancy here, would you?"

The clerk shook his head and replied, "The most amazing thing; someone just called in and canceled. We have one room available." Bob returned to the car to deliver the good news to Tammy, and we thanked God for the answered prayer. Considering this, and one other similar episode on an RV trip to see family, we now always reserve our stops.

Elroy-Sparta State Trail, Wisconsin

The next day we rode our tandem in Thompson Memorial Park on the Elroy-Sparta State Trail on crushed limestone. This took us through three preserved railway tunnels. We liked the area so much we stayed an extra day at the hotel and made certain we had reservations in Minneapolis, our next stop.

Breathtaking view, Yosemite National Park

In 2014, we flew to Seattle to visit Bob's sister Sue, husband Ken, and other relatives in the Seattle area. After brief visits, shared meals, and good conversation we began our trip down the Pacific Coast 101 Scenic Byway. There were many state parks and sites we did not have time to visit. Our planned itinerary included the Sequoia National Park, Redwood Forest, and Yosemite National Park. Immersed in the sequoias, we stepped out of our rented Impala to take a picture of us standing on the road under the tunnel log. Before returning to the car, Bob noticed a mid-sized black bear. Approximately 15-20 feet away, Tammy asked, "What are we going to do?" Bob said, "Remain calm, cross the road, and quietly walk back to the car." Tammy chose to not get out of the vehicle the remainder of the day except to tour the General Sherman Tree, the world's largest tree measured by volume.

Biking the Golden Gate Bridge

Our Pacific coast trip ended in San Francisco. As we toured the city, we were impressed with how many people were riding rented bicycles. From Fisherman's Wharf, Bob noticed bikers crossing the Golden Gate Bridge. This was not a planned bicycle trip, but a couple years into our biking journey, we did not want to pass up a golden opportunity to ride across the famous bridge. Stopping at Blazing Saddles, we were pleased to find they had a tandem bike available for rent. Biking this iconic bridge and riding the San Francisco trolley were two of our favorite memories of this city.

Butchart Gardens, a Canadian national treasure

We returned to Washington State in 2019 to bike on our tandem and to board a plane for our Alaska biking vacation. Before leaving for Alaska, we decided to add a day trip to Butchart Gardens in Victoria, British Columbia, a national historic site of Canada. Amazingly, these stunning gardens are still owned by the founding family, with the current owner being a great-granddaughter of the founding couple. We were on a time-limited excursion, but it was enough to witness the majestic beauty of the six gardens and to know this was a place to revisit in the future.

Clark Lake National Park, the second least visited national park

Previously, we mentioned the moose on the Tony Knowles Bike Trail in Juneau, but Alaska provided several other amazing adventures. Unlike the time we did not want to encounter a bear at Glacier National Park or the time we did encounter a bear at Sequoia National Park, in Alaska we boarded a small propeller plane to go on a guided, photography bear excursion. Tammy was able to photograph a mother bear and her cub from a safe distance with a guide and group of fellow photographers.

A picture-perfect shot

At the Alaska SeaLife Center in Seward, Tammy showed her phenomenal patience as she waited and shot multiple pictures of puffins for two hours until she got the perfect shot. She said, "These are the most hyperactive birds I've ever seen." As soon as she framed a shot they would quickly jump and jerk their heads. And Bob showed his unusual patience walking continuously around the center seeing many birds and animals native to Alaska while Tammy was in her element!

Our most challenging hike on the Alaska trip was at Prince William Sound on the Portage Pass Trail to see Portage Glacier. The loose gravel trail was steep and treacherous, but the view at the end of our trek was breathtaking. The scenery at the end of our hike included a crystal-clear stream, purple fireweed, yellow wildflowers, and a large, blue-toned glacier.

Chapter Twelve
IT'S NOT THE DESTINATION— IT'S THE JOURNEY

We accomplished our primary goal to bike in all fifty states and to have fun while doing it. While we have a sense of accomplishment in reaching this goal, in reflection, we realize the journey changed us. Along the way we learned about life, each other, and ourselves. Some of our reflections include:

1. There is always going to be another crisis. If we pray about the situation, don't lose our cool, and think creatively, we can overcome a lot of obstacles.

2. We feel rejuvenated when we get out of our ordinary routine. Traveling, exploring, and trying new things keeps us motivated and interested in life.

3. In life, the goals we most cherish often require great effort and a long period of time to accomplish.

4. Don't put off until tomorrow the important things you want to accomplish today because life can change in a moment.

5. The memories we create together and with family and friends are of far greater value than material things we possess.

6. We never know how much time we have left. We may not have the time, energy, or ability to go, see, and do in the future.

7. We work well as a team in ways we didn't expect.

8. We are good at making plans and are open to spontaneously adjusting them.

9. We have become more patient with each other, and we have learned to assume that our spouse has good intentions.

10. We believe in divine encounters. God places people in our lives, or us in their lives, at specific times for specific reasons.

11. Our faith continues to grow as we reflect on how God has carried us in the past, and we have confidence that he will in the future.

12. We know the importance of leaving a legacy of love and faith and are constantly thinking of ways to encourage and inspire others, especially our grandchildren.

CHRONOLOGICAL TANDEM BICYCLE ITINERARY

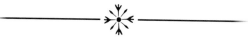

Massachusetts	8/14/2013	Martha's Vineyard
California	8/17/2014	Golden Gate Bridge, San Francisco
Michigan	5/06/2015	US Bicycle Route 35, Holland
Indiana	7/03/2015	Covered Bridge, Bridgeton
Wisconsin	7/18/2015	Elroy-Sparta Trail, Monroe County
Minnesota	7/20/2015	Chain of Lakes Loop, Minneapolis
Iowa	7/22/2015	Kewash Trail, Kalona
Missouri	7/23/2015	Hannibal
Illinois	7/24/2015	Route 66 Bike Route, Springfield
Maryland	7/13/2016	Columbia Maryland Trail System
Maine	7/16/2016	East Promenade Trail, Portland
New Hampshire	7/19/2016	Franconia Notch State Park
Vermont	7/20/2016	Covered Bridges, Bennington
New York	7/21/2016	Central Park, New York City
Pennsylvania	7/22/2016	Independence Square, Philadelphia
New Jersey	7/22/2016	Camden, New Jersey
Ohio	7/23/2016	Little Miami Scenic Trail
Kentucky	7/30/2017	Louisville Loop
Tennessee	7/31/2017	Music City Bike Trail, Nashville
Alabama	8/01/2017	Chief Ladiga Trail
Georgia	8/01/2017	Silver Comet Trail
South Carolina	8/02/2017	Hilton Head Island
North Carolina	8/05/2017	Ocracoke Island, Outer Banks
Virginia	8/06/2017	High Bridge Trail, Farmville

West Virginia	8/07/2017	Mon River Trail, Morgantown
Nebraska	7/21/2018	Fort Kearney Hike-Bike Trail
Wyoming	7/23/2018	Grand Teton National Park
Idaho	7/26/2018	Hiawatha Trail
Montana	7/27/2018	Glacier National Park
North Dakota	7/30/2018	Patterson Park, Dickinson
South Dakota	8/01/2018	Badlands National Park
Delaware	10/08/2018	Delaware City Branch Canal Trail
Connecticut	10/10/2018	Farmington Canal Heritage Trail
Rhode Island	10/11/2018	Cranston Trail
Colorado	7/03/2019	Poudre River Trail, Fort Collins
Oregon	7/06/2019	Kelley Point Park, Portland
Washington	7/07/2019	Columbia River Renaissance Trail
Alaska	7/10/2019	Tony Knowles Coastal Trail
Louisiana	9/03/2019	Tammany Trace Trail
Mississippi	9/05/2019	Longleaf Trace Trail
Arkansas	9/06/2019	Arkansas River Trail
Florida	7/21/2020	Pensacola Beach
Hawaii	2/17/2021	Banyan Tree Park, Lahaina
Texas	4/16/2022	Salado Greenway Trail, San Antonio
New Mexico	4/21/2022	White Sands National Park
Arizona	4/23/2022	The Loop Trail, Tucson
Nevada	4/30/2022	River Mountain Loop Trail
Utah	5/04/2022	Moab Canyon Trail
Oklahoma	5/09/2022	Tulsa River Parks Trail
Kansas	5/11/2022	Overland Park Bike/Hike Trail

Printed in the United States
by Baker & Taylor Publisher Services